WHO WAS...

ST FRANCIS OF ASSISI

The Patron Saint of Animals

LUCY LETHBRIDGE

Illustrations by Alex Fox

* SHORT BOOKS

First published in 2005 by

Short Books

15 Highbury Terrace

London N5 1UP

10 9 8 7 6 5 4 3 2 1

A CIP catalogue record for this book
is available from the British Library.

Illustration copyright © Alex Fox 2005

Quiz by Sebastian Blake

ISBN 1-904977-17-0

Printed and bound in Great Britain by
Bookmarque Ltd., Croydon, Surrey

ST FRANCIS OF ASSISI

For Bea Marston, Anna Curzon-Price, Tiggy Elwes,
Alexander Adams, Thomas Jackson, Thomas Lethbridge
and Molly Lywood.

It was a blisteringly hot afternoon in the valley of Spoleto. The city of Assisi, clinging to its steep hillside, baked silently in the sun. Flea-bitten cats and dogs stretched out, panting, on the hot cobbles, and a shimmering haze hung over the terraced slopes below the town. In the great plain between the hills, even the river looked static, as though it were too exhausted to flow. All the citizens of Assisi were indoors, resting in the cool of their stone houses, but had one of them been leaning over the city walls in the brilliant stillness, he would have spotted a figure on the road which skirted the base of the mountain; he would have heard the distant clang of a leper's bell.

Far below, the leper had no sensation in his feet, so

he couldn't feel the burning dust of the road. Leprosy deadens flesh: the sufferer's nerves freeze up and he loses all feeling; eventually his nose, toes and fingers drop off. The leper's lips were swollen and parched and his thin tunic flapped against his blotched body. His face was distorted by large nut-like protuberances. A leather bag and a wooden bowl hung from his belt. He'd had a disappointing day's begging. He was very hungry but if he stopped under a bush to rest, he would only fall asleep and wake up still hungry. His bell felt very heavy today, but he clanged it dutifully – it was forbidden by law for lepers to go outside without ringing bells to warn people of their approach. Sometimes passers-by threw loose change on the ground in front of him, then ran off with their cloaks over their mouths or holding their noses. Not only was leprosy infectious, but sufferers gave off an unpleasant, goatish, smell.

Clang, clang, clang, went the leper's bell. He hardly heard the thundering of

8

the horse's hooves as they tore down the hairpin bends from Assisi. He looked up, then backed off a little, keeping his head bent. He knew, as all lepers in those days knew, that people didn't like coming near him. If he stood still, it gave the rider the opportunity to throw something on the ground: a crust of bread perhaps; if he were lucky he might get a coin. So he waited, his eyes lowered.

For a few seconds nothing happened, the horse pounded the ground, snorting: the rider seemed to be waiting, pausing, thinking. The leper raised his eyes tentatively. He saw a riding boot in soft leather, a flash of brightly-coloured cloak, an expensive whip. He raised his eyes further and there was a slight, dark, young man with thick black eyebrows that formed a bar across his forehead. The leper sighed with relief: it was young Francis Bernadone, the rich merchant's son from Assisi. Light-hearted, laughing and idle, Francis was always generous; everybody liked Francis. But the leper knew that Francis, too, was frightened: he had many times before seen disgust and fear in his eyes. Still, Francis was always good for a penny or two, so the leper crouched and waited.

The horse's bridle jangled as the young man jumped lightly to the ground. Then Francis walked towards the leper, pulling violently at his leather purse as though he wanted to be rid of it. It came loose and he held it out in front of him. He didn't throw it on the ground, but he held it out to the leper as though it were a gift from friend to friend. The leper hardly dared look, but he reached out and took the purse, which felt heavy with coins. Then, as the leper pulled the gold back towards himself, Francis Bernadone's hand clasped his hand. It had been so long since anyone had touched the leper that he shivered as if in fear. This was so strange. Bernadone came nearer, and the leper felt the cool shade of his shadow. Seconds later, the young man pressed his lips on the leper's diseased hands. The leper's hands had no feeling left in them, but he knew that this was a kiss.

CHAPTER 1
The Beginning

Francis Bernadone was 24 years old when he kissed the leper. It was the turning point of his life. Twenty years later, on his deathbed, when he and his thousands of followers had sent waves of change across Europe, Francis said that it was at that moment that his life had changed forever. Kissing a leper's hands might not seem to us today such a very courageous thing to do. But nine hundred years ago, in the time when Francis lived, before doctors knew the causes of illnesses like leprosy, lepers were terrifying figures, outcasts shunned by ordinary people who thought that they might die if they went near one. Kissing a leper was a mad thing to do: only in a world turned upside down did a healthy person choose to kiss a leper.

But that is what makes St Francis of Assisi so important: he was a revolutionary, telling people that they could only be happy if they made friends with the people that they most feared and despised; if they actually gave away all their money and possessions, rather than trying to amass more. Thousands of people now visit Assisi, which is in Tuscany, in the centre of Italy, to see where St Francis lived. Built into the mountainside, there is a vast church dedicated to him which can be seen from far across the valley. Inside, wonderful paintings tell the story of his extraordinary life. They show a smallish, bearded, barefoot man in a rough robe. In one picture, he is shown speaking to a flock of birds; in another he gives his cloak to a beggar. In all of them, the painter has tried to capture the look of sweetness in Francis's face – as well as his determination. Francis had once been called mad but he saw the world more clearly than anyone else. After St Francis of Assisi, politics, religion, and the way that people thought about the world around them, would not be the same again.

***

Francis was born in 1181, in Assisi. He was the son of a wealthy cloth merchant called Pietro Bernadone and his wife Giovanna, known as Pica. They christened their baby not Francis but Giovanni. Young Giovanni from an early age loved the songs that his father picked up during his business trips to the glittering trade fairs of France. They were the songs of travelling minstrels and poets known as troubadours: love songs and ballads of courtly love, knights, hidden treasure, castles and beautiful princesses. In Assisi, young Giovanni liked to show-off the snatches of rough French that his father taught him. 'Il Francesco' the Bernadone's neighbours shouted after him teasingly when they heard him singing in the street. Il Francesco (in English Francis), means 'the Frenchman' and the name stuck. From childhood onwards, he was always known as Francis.

Francis's mother was a meek figure, flattened by the loud bluster of her husband. Pica wanted to protect Francis from his father's rages. Pietro often yelled at him, complained that his his head was full of 'romantic rubbish' and that he showed no inclination to work hard at his Latin studies. But he was secretly proud of Francis's charm: he was popular in a way which his hard-working, gruff father had never been. And he soon had a gang of friends in Assisi – the sons of noble-men. Pietro Bernadone, Assisi's most prosperous merchant, purveyor of the finest silks and velvets to the grandest families in the city, had never felt as though they treated him as their equal. Yet Francis was as light-hearted with these lazy young nobles as he was with everybody else. Years later, in one of the many chronicles of the life of Francis, someone who knew him at this time described his voice as particularly beautiful: 'powerful, sweet-toned, clear and sonorous'.

Francis was always playing games, dancing or idling around with his friends. Of all the gangs of young men who tore about the streets of Assisi, Francis belonged to the one which seemed to be always having the most fun. He was cheerful, easy-going, amusing and everybody wanted to invite him to their parties. He enjoyed pranks, and practical jokes and teasing – but he wasn't cruel. His father thought he should knuckle down and think of his future in the cloth business. It was a prosperous trade but merchants had to work hard, spending weeks and months away from home. Every year, Pietro Bernadone travelled to France, to cloth fairs where the finest, softest material could be bought. In the main square there was a busy market where Pietro had a stall selling velvets, silks and finely woven wool.

There were occasions when Francis's behaviour was extremely odd. Once, when he was left in charge of

Pietro's stall, he had given a poor woman a length of cloth and refused to take a penny for it; in fact he had jumped over the tables in the market, in front of everyone, and raced after her, holding the cloth above his head before handing it over with a bow. 'It's only money,' he said when his father returned and flew into a rage. 'Only money,'

Pietro shouted, 'Only money! It's money, hard-earned through my graft, that enables you to snooze

your afternoons away dreaming of romances, and it's my money which buys you those fashionable clothes you like so much, and it's my money which you hand out so lavishly to all your friends.'

But even Pietro had to admit, sheepishly, that it had been generous of Francis to give the cloth to the poor woman. Those noble knights, those chevaliers, in Francis's French songs would surely have done the same. Pietro didn't know whether to admire the action or despise it. One thing was all too obvious: Francis was never going to be a successful merchant.

The priests of Assisi were not happy with Francis either. He didn't do any work and they strongly disapproved of those love songs. 'Time-wasting' his teachers muttered as they heard him clattering down the cobbles to his lessons, late as usual. He might even – horrors! – have been singing too, something like this:

Take, O Rose, this Rose
It is the flower of love,
And by this very Rose,
I captive am of love

If Pietro Bernadone feared that Francis would ruin the family with his carefree attitude to spending money, the priests thought that he was sliding headlong down the slippery slope that led to hell – a fiery pit full of squanderers, idlers, dancers and other layabouts.

At the time of Francis's birth, the Spoleto Valley, in which Assisi was situated, was ruled by a German, Duke Conrad of Urslingen, who had been given control of the region in recognition of his services to the Holy Roman Empire – which then ruled most of Italy. But by 1198, when Francis was 17, that empire had grown weak and, in Rome, a new pope had been elected who wanted to take back many of the lands under the Empire's control. One day, Duke Conrad and the citizens of Assisi watched as the forces of Pope Innocent III gathered in the valley. Knowing they were outnumbered, Conrad rode his men out of the valley and surrendered his lands to the Pope.

The immediate result of the departure of Duke Conrad was violence between the citizens of Assisi themselves. The middle classes, which included merchants like Pietro Bernadone, resented the special privileges and hereditary rights that were claimed by the aristocratic families in the city – purely because of their grand birth – and they rose up in protest. The grandest houses were torched or pulled down and most of the nobles fled to the neighbouring city of Perugia.

Assisi was now led by businessmen, the hard-working merchants who had earned the money which had made the city wealthy. But in Perugia the exiled noblemen, many of whose sons were Francis's friends, simmered and waited for their chance to take revenge on Assisi.

Two years after their flight to Perugia, the Assisian nobles joined forces with the Perugians and launched an attack on their home town. They were enthusiastic soldiers as they had been promised rich pickings and the restoration of all their properties if Perugia was victorious.

Most of Pope Innocent III's soldiers were away fighting in other areas of the country, and Assisi was left undefended. When the citizens heard news of the impending attack, they had no choice but to arm themselves and try and hold off the Perugians as best they could. Francis was excited: it had been his dream to be a soldier (though he had always seen himself as more the swooning knight who rescues the princess than a battle-scarred fighter).

Amid the panic, the hasty boarding-up of doors, and the stockpiling of flour and clean water, the Bernadones wondered if the battle might be the making of Francis, the challenge that he needed to grow into a man. Pietro kitted his son out with the finest armour, and a glossy horse. Francis rode to war in high spirits but he was captured in the very first skirmish. He'd barely had time to draw his shining new sword.

The captured Assisian soldiers were divided up and thrown into different dungeons in Perugia Castle. In one lay the poorest foot soldiers, those who didn't have enough money to make them important to the Perugians: they were forced into slave labour. In the other dungeon, in more comfortable conditions, were Francis and others whose fathers could afford to pay a hefty ransom for their freedom. They didn't have to do hard labour, but instead had to wile away hours of boredom in the dimly-lit prison cells.

Soon Francis's relentless cheer began to grate on his fellow prisoners' nerves. They muttered about him among themselves: he simply did not see how serious their situation was. They were locked up in a dungeon, with rats chewing their hair at night, with their enemies waiting for the chance to execute them, and Francis just kept on smiling. As the months went by, they wondered if he was not quite right in the head. Many years later, when Francis was the most famous Assisian who had ever lived, several of the prisoners remembered how they asked him why he was so happy: then he had replied: 'Why am I happy? Because one day the world will reverence me.' No wonder Assisian prisoners were irritated. How were they to know that Francis Bernadone would become a saint?

***

After just under two years in captivity, Francis was set free. He was 21 years old, and his father probably paid a large sum for his release. He returned to find Assisi a changed city. The noble families had one by one returned to their former properties (or what was left of them) but now under new, fairer conditions which gave the merchants, men like Pietro Bernadone, a lot more say in the running of the city. The nobles realised that from now on they would be sharing their power with prosperous traders – the very people that they had before considered too lowly even to consult about government.

The cloth trade was flourishing and the Bernadones were richer than ever. To his father's disappointment, Francis threw himself energetically into his old life of partying late into the night, then getting up late in the morning, usually with a throbbing hangover. He good-naturedly agreed to help his father on his stall in the cloth fair, but he couldn't disguise the fact that his heart wasn't in it. More often than not, Pietro would leave the stall for a few hours and come back to find Francis dozing on a pile of expensive cloth. On one occasion, he wandered off to chat to a friend or take a stroll – and then forgot to come back. 'He just FORGOT!' bawled a despairing Pietro Bernadone to his wife. The merchant had hoped prison might have taught his son to take life more seriously, but Francis was all too obviously still his laid-back old self.

Then, about 18 months after his homecoming, Francis fell seriously ill. It might have been due to his liver – and too much heavy drinking – or it might have been another illness altogether. Whatever it was, Francis had to stay in bed for several weeks. During this period, as he later told other people, who then told others who wrote it down (which is the way that most of our information about Francis comes down the centuries to us), he wrestled hard with himself. Forced into a long period of reflection without the usual fug of a hangover, he pondered on his life. What on earth was he going to do with himself? How should he find a point to his life? What was he, Francis Bernadone, here on earth to do?

When he was finally well enough to get out of bed, the weakened Francis took long walks around the vineyards leaning on a cane. He seemed listless and depressed. But at least he was thinking about his future: 'I'm going to be a soldier,' he announced to his parents. Pietro and Pica looked doubtful: they remembered Francis's previous attempt to be a military hero. Pietro tried to interest him, again, in the cloth business, but Francis wouldn't even listen to him. 'I don't want to take money from people and spend my days squinting over account books. I want a life which has some glory in it.'

Later, he looked back over this time and said he'd had 'visions of great renown' – which is a flowery way of saying that he had pictured himself being famous and admired. For the first time since Francis had returned from Perugia, Pietro looked hard at his son. His eyes now seemed withdrawn and faraway. He wondered if perhaps Francis had gone a bit, well, crazy.

Pietro Bernadone was not, however, a man of half-measures. When he decided to do something he did it properly. If Francis really wanted to be a soldier, he would make sure the lad departed Assisi the best-dressed, and best equipped soldier, the city had ever set eyes on. Francis had dreams of being a Crusader – which was the name given to the Christian soldiers who went to Palestine to fight the Arabs (known then as

Saracens) who had taken control of Jerusalem about 20 years before. Crusaders were the inspiration behind the knightly virtues in the French songs that Francis loved. To him (and to most people in Christian Europe at that time) there could be no higher cause than fighting for the return of the Holy Places.

Going on a Crusade was no easy matter, however, and it was probably a good idea to first get some fighting practice in a battle closer to home. Francis learned that a nobleman of Assisi was leading a military expedition to southern Italy – probably in support of the Pope's armies against the Germans who were still there. He enlisted to join them and duly set out adorned in the finest armour on another magnificent horse, and accompanied by his own shield bearer. He intended to win his spurs and return home a knight who had fought for honour.

But, of course, this being Francis, events did not go according to plan. In a matter of days he had returned to Assisi. The truth was that he got only as far as the town of Spoleto before he turned the glittering bridle of his horse and came back.

No one knows for certain what happened to Francis in Spoleto. Some accounts of this period of his life say he had a dream that his bedroom was filled with the weapons of war. In those days dreams were taken very seriously as glimpses of the future and Francis took this to be a warning. According to other stories, he had a vision in which he heard the voice of God, asking him, 'Who is it better to serve, the servant or the master?' (The answer of course is that God is the real master and the leaders of military campaigns are servants who have no real power.) Another story suggests that Francis met a poor knight on the road and in a rush of generosity handed over his armour and clothing in exchange for the knight's ragged cloak.

We will never know exactly what happened – all of these stories sound typical of Francis in different ways – but the result was that Francis looked deep into his heart and realised that he could never be a soldier. So he returned to Assisi to face the scorn and amazement of his family and friends. Francis acted just as impulsively when he did not want to do something as when he did want to do something.

***

Pietro could hardly believe his eyes when he heard that dusty, hungry Francis had appeared on the road towards the city. Francis Bernadone, once the most popular boy in Assisi, was now a figure of fun. When he got home, his mother wrung her hands; his father couldn't speak to him at all, but eyeballed him furiously. The peculiar thing was that Francis didn't seem ashamed, cowed or embarrassed. He wasn't light-hearted in the way that he had been before, but pensive and quiet. These days no one could be quite sure what mood he was going to be in. He wasn't moody in a grumpy sort of way; it was just that he was always saying things that took people by surprise.

He took to going on long rides and walks on his own, pounding through the chestnut woods for many hours. He began to look closely at his world, the world he had lived in all his life, and every day he saw it in a fresh light. He'd always been comfortable, warm, well-fed, but now he saw clearly the beggars, the lepers, the poor and the lonely.

One day, without warning, he announced that he was going to live in a cave in the mountains with a close friend. This was not so uncommon in the Middle Ages: people saw intense solitude as a way of getting close to God without distractions or in order to prepare oneself for a momentous change in one's life. Some of the gossips of Assisi speculated that Francis might even be thinking of getting married.

A month later, when he returned from the cave, his friends made him 'King of the Revels' which was a

title given to the most madcap party-lover in the town. But by that time, they must have been teasing because it was clear that Francis was no longer interested in parties. He seemed distracted, light-headed – like a man in love. The friend who had accompanied him to the cave told them that Francis had indeed confided to him that he wanted to be married. But – guess what? – his bride was not going to be a flesh and blood woman at all but poverty itself. Francis Bernadone called his future bride 'My Lady

Poverty' and she came without money or possessions. She was joyful and light and unburdened.

For the people of Assisi, it was proof, if proof were needed, that Francis had gone off his head completely. When his father heard about this Lady Poverty nonsense he snapped completely, and tried to provoke a row. But Francis, happy, separate, in his own world, seemed not to mind what other people thought of him. Assisi had strict codes about what was considered respectable behaviour and Francis appeared to care not one jot about any of them. Which brings the story up to the moment when he cantered down a blindingly hot road and pulled his horse to a halt before the cringing figure of the most unwanted, least respectable, person in his world – thc leper.

CHAPTER 2
The madman of Assisi

Pietro Bernadone was in a towering rage. His son was stark, staring mad, insane. 'He kissed a leper' he shouted to his wife. 'He put his lips to his skin and actually kissed him!'

She looked nervous and wrung her hands. 'Are you sure that's true? It would be such a very foolish thing to do – he might catch something.'

'I wouldn't be standing here telling you about it if it weren't true. I had it from a cloth buyer in the market, and he had it from one of the nuns from the leprosaria who actually had it from the leper Francis kissed. Apparently they're all talking about it. And what is more, since then he's been visiting the leprosaria, talking to lepers and, would you believe it, washing their

28

feet!' Pietro thought Francis's behaviour grotesque. He thought he was showing off, deliberately trying to make his father look a fool in front of all his customers. What had Pietro ever done to him? He'd worked all his life so his son could dance, sing and play silly games with the young men of the city. Francis was 24, he should be married, working, being an ordinary, law-abiding Christian citizen who remembered to give the odd coin to the less well-off. Instead, he was a loser, a waster, a no-good lunatic who kissed lepers. He dishonoured the name of Bernadone.

Pica was frightened: something was happening to Francis and she did not, could not, understand what it was. He was so peculiar, so different. She felt sure he was losing his mind. She pictured him wandering through the rest of his life: mad, lonely, talking to himself, with no one to protect him from the taunts of the world. What is more, she felt sure it was just the beginning.

Then it came. The moment they dreaded.

Francis left the house early one morning for a long walk. He passed one of Assisi's little churches, just outside the town. San Damiano was dilapidated and Francis stopped to chat, as he often did, with the old priest who looked after it; the priest told him how he had to watch it grow more decrepit every year because there was no money for repairs. Francis looked at the church as if he was seeing it for the first time. He went inside, and knelt before the painted wooden crucifix on the altar. In the silence, he heard the figure of Jesus on the Cross speaking to him quite clearly. His words were, 'Rebuild my church'. It is typical of Francis that he immediately leapt to a conclusion, without stopping to puzzle over which church he was to rebuild. Those words may, after all, have meant that Francis was destined to change the face of the whole institution of the Church. But, for now, he thought its message was more straightforward: he had to rebuild San Damiano. He said goodbye to the startled priest and ran back up to the town.

Then, knowing his father was away on business, he unlocked Pietro's shop and took down two rolls of expensive cloth. He saddled up his horse and rode to Foligno to sell the cloth for as much money as he could. But before he left, he did an interesting thing: he chalked on his tunic a Cross like the one that crusaders wore on their armour when they rode to battle. From now on, Francis saw himself as a knight riding out to help the poor. Clutching the money he had earned in Foligno, he rode at breakneck speed back to San

Damiano and presented it to the priest.

The priest must have been amazed: it was not unusual for the rich to give money to churches but this young man, son of Assisi's wealthiest merchant, had given him the purse as if he could hardly bear to touch it; he threw it away from him as though the money was poisoned. The priest was disturbed, too, by the fact that the gold had effectively been stolen from Pietro Bernadone. He refused to spend it and put it in a safe place for the moment when Francis would have to return it.

At which Francis decided to get back at his father in the most effective way possible: he vowed that for the rest of his life he would never again touch money – not so much as a single coin.

CHAPTER 3
Naked in the town square

Francis stayed at San Damiano for more than two weeks, sleeping in the priest's hut and looking at the stars through holes in the roof. During the day, he helped rebuild the church himself. His clothes got dirty and tattered, he ate simple food and got wet when it rained. But he liked the feeling of not always being comfortable; it made him feel alive and alert. He needed to be alert because he was listening, waiting to hear what God wanted him to do next. This wasn't quite all: he also always kept an ear open to listen out for his father. Terrified of the punishment that awaited him when he was discovered, he built a pit in the bemused priest's garden in which, he explained, he would hide when Pietro came looking for him.

Finally, of course, Pietro did find out where his son was, and rushed down to San Damiano in a storming fury. Francis lay crouched in his pit, and the priest pretended not to know where he was. Francis stayed in the pit a whole month then, typically, one day, without warning, he just decided to go back to the town and face his father. He walked up the hill to Assisi. His clothes were filthy, his hair was matted, he had a straggly beard. As he approached, the townspeople pelted him with stones and mud, shouting 'il pazzo, il pazzo!' which means 'madman'. Pietro, speechless with humiliation, Pica weeping behind him, went to meet him in the town square and dragged him home. He locked him fast in the cellar of the house, chained to a ring in the wall. His mother brought him food and begged him to apologise but Francis refused.

'The boy is mad. He'll be imprisoned until he is sane again,' shouted Pietro. The two men were like stubborn bulls snorting in a ring, each refusing to give an inch. One day, after a few weeks, while Pietro was out of the house, Pica, unable to bear it any longer, let Francis out.

What did he do then? Naturally, he did the one thing that his father didn't want him to do: he went back to San Damiano and continued breaking stones to repair the church walls. And, naturally, when Pietro returned he immediately went down to the church and dragged Francis back home again. The moment his back was turned, Francis went back to San Damiano. And so it went on. Finally, Pietro decided to resort to the law. Under the law of the state, the punishment for stealing your father's property and disobeying him, as Francis had done, was banishment. The judge's messenger rode out to San Damiano to deliver the sentence – which was that Francis leave the Spoleto Valley that very day and never come back. Francis barely looked up from his work, saying only: 'Your letter does not concern me. I am no longer interested in the power of your law as I am attached to this church as a servant of God.'

***

It was quite true: by living and working at San Damiano, Francis had removed himself from the power of the judges and was now under the protection of the Church. Pietro had no choice but to ask for help from the only authority in Assisi that Francis recognised: the Bishop. He demanded that Francis stand up in front of the Bishop, outside the cathedral, and renounce his inheritance. Francis was not remotely interested in his inheritance, which came to a great deal of money, but in those days, for a father to disinherit his son was a huge scandal. Imagine if your father said, in public, that he no longer loved you or wanted to have anything to do with you ever again, and had no intention of ever letting you have any of his money. Francis agreed to let it happen because he wanted to be free.

And so, on 5 February 1207, watched by crowds of fascinated Assisians, a bedraggled Francis and a splendidly-dressed Pietro stood up together before the Cathedral of Santa Maggiore. The Bishop stood on the steps above them wearing his richly-embroidered vestments and his mitre. He declared that Francis should pay his father back the money he had earned from selling the cloth as it would be wrong to rebuild the church with the proceeds from stolen goods. Not only did Francis renounce his rights, he publicly denounced his very own father. And in a spectacularly dramatic fashion. He tore off all his clothes and flung them on the ground; then on top of them he threw the bag of money he owed Pietro.

'I want nothing from my father,' he cried. There he stood, stark naked, having stripped away not only his clothes but all his old life. Now he owned nothing –

and he was free. But it was a terribly cruel way to treat his own father. His son had made a fool of him in front of the entire city, and as he shuffled forward to pick up the money Pietro's cheeks burned with shame.

The crowd was silent and uncomfortable as Francis stood before them in the icy February air – a thin, dirty figure, his brown skin scratched by the brambles and stones of San Damiano. The Bishop whispered to his

servant that he should cover this strange creature with a cloak, and before they wrapped it around him, Francis chalked on it another large cross – the symbol of Jesus Christ that Crusaders wore into battle. 'I am taking the Cross,' he announced to his assembled listeners, 'From now on, I am a crusader for the poor.' What could they say? Some people, probably the poor ones, cheered; others looked away, embarrassed on behalf of the Bernadones and their half-wit son. A few probably laughed: there hadn't been a drama as good as this one in Assisi for years.

***

So Francis left his home town wearing only a peasant's thin tunic (the bishop had hastily retrieved his warm cloak before this peculiar young man could walk off with it). He was entirely alone, but he had discovered something about being naked: it felt absolutely free; the people could laugh and scorn him all they wanted: their taunts only brought him closer to God who was the source of everything that was real and true. It was the beginning of his new life, and he was completely happy.

CHAPTER 4
The wanderer

This time, as Francis again walked down the hill from Assisi, he had no idea where he was going. He was cold, hungry and in search of adventure. He was looking for something though he didn't yet know what it was. He just knew he had to keep walking until he found out.

The raggle-taggle, itchy-footed life of the wanderer suited Francis. In the thirteenth century, it was quite common to live by roaming from place to place. Francis would have been just one among the throngs of travelling musicians, soldiers, tramps, beggars, preachers, minstrels, gypsies and pilgrims that would have passed through Assisi and other towns in the hope of a bed for the night and a hot meal.

According to those who catch the wandering bug, one of the chief pleasures of life on the road is not knowing what will happen the next day. Francis's policy was to put his trust in God, knowing that he was always looked after. As he contemplated his new life, he was so filled with excitement that he began to sing. He was singing so lustily while passing through a thick forest that he was unaware of the band of robbers behind him until they pinned his arms behind his back and asked him who he was. Francis replied, 'I am the herald of the Great King' – by which he meant he was a messenger of God, sent to tell the world of a wonderful way of being close to goodness. The robbers must have been a bit surprised, and when it was obvious that he had no money they punched him hard and threw him into a ditch full of snow, shouting 'Lie there you peasant herald!'.

After they had gone Francis jumped out of the ditch and, alone among the leafless trees, his face splotched with a purple bruise, sang out his joy in God who had created the beautiful, wintry woodland. As thousands of people were soon to learn, you never got quite the reaction you expected from Francis Bernadone.

For his first night of freedom, Francis was taken in by monks in a nearby monastery. He stayed there for several days, working in the kitchens. But he was soon restless, wanting to be on the move again. He packed up, put on the old tunic in which he had arrived and set off down the road. When he was hungry he begged for bread; sometimes a kind person would give him some cooked meat or an apple, and when he was tired, he knocked at a door and sometimes was offered a bed for the night; if there was no bed, he curled up under a bush and slept on the frost-bitten ground.

Before long Francis arrived at the town of Gubbio, 40 miles or so from Assisi. The hills beyond Gubbio marked completely new territory; it was the beginning of the rest of the world. In Gubbio he looked up an old crony from his party-going days – Count Spadalunga. The Count must have been amazed to see his friend Francis, string-thin and wearing filthy clothes but smiling broadly. But he gave him a bed and found him a job in a leprosaria.

Francis had been in Gubbio for several months when he made another of his surprising, on-the-spur-of-the-moment decisions: to go home to Assisi. It seems curious that on the brink of a new adventure, he wilfully decided to return to the looming shadow of his father and the taunts of the Assisians. But his mind was made up and he walked happily back to Assisi with a plan to restore all the many ruined churches in the city. He would scrape off the moss, lovingly replace the mortar between the cracked stones, and fill the churches again with singing congregations of people.

He began with San Damiano, lodging in a nearby hostel for lepers. He immediately set to work, although he knew nothing about stonemasonry. He wanted to learn and, anyway, he was sure that he was doing what God wanted and that God would show him the way. And it seemed that God did, because gradually the churches came to life again.

With no money to pay for materials, Francis literally had to beg for the very stones he needed. He walked into the city in his rags, under the nose of his affronted father, and stopped people to ask them to give him stones and oil to keep the churches' lamps alight. Most people in Assisi had seen enough of Francis Bernadone and his mad ideas, but he persevered, and when they saw him lugging the stones down the hill to San Damiano, they saw he was serious. He chipped away at the stones all day, and when there was enough moonlight he worked all night too.

He also begged for food for himself. From their kitchen windows, cooks gave him meagre scrapings from the bottom of their pans. And Francis proclaimed

41

those bits the most delicious food in the world.

For Pietro, Francis's begging was the final degradation. The Bernadone table was groaning with food: Francis only had to ask for it, to apologise and return to the family which loved him despite everything he had done to them. But Pietro was as obstinate as his son, and, of course, he couldn't say anything when he encountered Francis in the street – instead, he swore at him and turned away.

Then Francis did another cruel thing. He enlisted the help of an old beggar in the town and promised him a share of his begging bowl if the old man would follow him about like a shadow. Whenever they met Pietro, Francis would ostentatiously turn to the old beggar and say 'Bless me father'; the old man then made the Sign of the Cross over him as though he were Francis's father rather than Pietro. This was Francis's way of telling his father that he meant nothing to him. One day, Francis turned to his father in the street, pointed at the old beggar and said to Pietro: 'Do you not realise that God can give me a father whose blessings will counter your curses?' It was the last time the two men ever spoke to one another.

When San Damiano was fully repaired, Francis threw his energies into another church – the dilapidated chapel of San Pietro della Spina. No sooner was that restored than he came upon another ruin, hidden in the woods at the base of the mountain. Its name was St Mary of the Angels (because it was said that angels could be heard singing there) but was also known as the Portiuncula. For Francis it became the most important of all Assisi's churches. Day and night he worked on the church and when it was completed, the roof secure and the oil-lamps burning, a priest came

down from an abbey in the mountains to say Mass. It was February 1208 – almost exactly one year after Francis had renounced his father; he was now 27.

Francis listened to the priest intently, particularly when he read the bit from St Matthew's Gospel in which Jesus tells his followers to go out into the world without money or possessions. Most people would think that Francis was already doing just that, but the moment he heard those words, he sprang up, ready for action. He was always listening out for inspiration, for God whispering in his heart, telling him what to do next. 'This is what I want,' he cried out at the end of the Mass, 'this is what I long for with all my heart'.

Francis had never paused to think before he acted, and this occasion was no exception. He just couldn't wait to get started. First of all, he made himself a kind of uniform: a very rough and scratchy grey tunic which he wore over breeches; he looped a rope belt around his waist; as before, he marked his tunic with a Cross. He threw away his leather sandals and his walking stick. Then he stood at the foot of the road to Assisi, where travellers turned upwards towards the city, and he began to preach, quoting the words that had changed his life: 'If you wish to be perfect, go, sell all your possessions, and give the money to the poor'.

CHAPTER 5
New companions

Francis's new life was so extreme, uncomfortable and difficult that you wouldn't have thought many people would want to live in the way he did. Yet one of the interesting things about the story of Francis of Assisi is how attractive he made the prospect of owning nothing at all. From the moment that he stood on the road to Assisi in his distinctive grey tunic, his eyes blazing with enthusiasm, passers-by would stop, listen and think about what he said. The next day they quite often came back to hear more. Francis had taken Jesus's words so literally that he didn't even have a stick to lean on, but he still possessed the charming, light-hearted manner and the musical voice that had once crowned him 'The King of the Revels'.

One day in spring, two or three months after Francis had heard the words of the Gospel in the Portiuncula, a man – a few years older than Francis – pressed some bread into his bowl. Then he sat down on the rough ground and listened closely to what this unkempt, barefoot figure was saying. The man was richly dressed, a merchant by the looks of him; if he were to sell everything he possessed, it would amount to a lot of stuff. The man came back the next day and the next. He said his name was Bernard Quintavalle and he invited Francis to come up to his house in Assisi and have supper with him.

***

Bernard was a quiet, thoughtful type, and when they sat together, he let Francis do most of the talking in his burning-eyed, excitable way. Then Bernard asked him this question: 'If a man is given many possessions and has enjoyed them for several years, and now wants to get rid of them – what do you think he should do?' Of course, Francis knew exactly what this question meant. This man wanted to join Francis, to give away everything he owned and take to the freedom of the road. Francis had made his first convert.

The next morning, Bernard and Francis walked round Assisi giving every one of Bernard's possessions away to beggars, orphans and lepers. Then they went to the cathedral and picked up the Bible. It fell open at that very passage from St Matthew's Gospel, 'If you wish to be perfect, go sell your possessions and give your money to the poor.' It was a sign! They opened the Bible at another page and there were the words, 'Take nothing for your journey, neither staff, nor wallet, nor bread, nor money.' When they opened it the third time, they read this: 'If any man will follow me, let him deny himself and take up his cross and follow me.' There could be no going back now.

Some people were appalled. It was one thing for Francis Bernadone to take off his clothes and preach at street corners, but it was quite another for Bernard Quintavalle, that respectable merchant, to go off to join him in his topsy-turvy world where everything was the wrong way up. Bernard should be making money, not giving it away to every whining rag-tag who asked for it.

The two men built themselves a rough hut out of willow branches, down in the woods near the Portiuncula. They took care not to make the hut too comfortable and slept on stones instead of pillows. It wasn't long before they were joined by others. A man called Peter and a farm labourer called Giles came to find them. Francis took Giles into Assisi to beg for some cloth to make him a grey tunic and on their way, they met a beggar woman. Giles gave her the shabby coat off his back and Francis, delighted, said that at that moment he saw a wonderful vision of Giles and his coat flying merrily up to heaven.

***

Francis soon set off roaming again and took Giles with him. Later, Giles recalled how Francis had sung French love songs along the way. They stopped at castles, villages and towns where they preached and told people how they were on a romantic quest for perfection. Sometimes they were laughed out of town but often people stopped and listened. It was hurtful though that girls often ran away from them, scared off by the sight of their blackened feet and filthy hair. When they got back home, they found that three more companions had joined Peter and Bernard in the cabin in the woods. Francis called each of them by the name of 'brother' – the group had become a brotherhood.

The brothers' lives revolved round three activities:

praying, begging and preaching. It is not easy to learn to be a beggar. For one thing, it is extremely embarrassing. But Francis insisted that it was actually as joyful to beg for food as it was to give food to someone who needed it. When people complained that there were far too many beggars in the world he retorted that, on the contrary, there weren't nearly enough. He sent the brothers out into neighbouring villages with instructions to beg only for what food they needed for that day. After a while they became quite competitive,

peering in each other's bowls to see how successful they had been. 'Do not worry about tomorrow', Francis liked to quote these words of Jesus when they fretted.

The only thing they were absolutely forbidden to beg for was money. Once a generous benefactor left a bag of coins in the church for them and one of the brothers stored it away thinking it might come in useful. When Francis heard about this, he was furious. He couldn't bear to touch the gold himself and ordered the offending brother to pick up the money in his mouth then drop it in the nearest dung-heap.

***

The brothers' preaching tour that summer had a mixed response. They were mocked, teased, and in many villages the inhabitants thought from their appearance that they were wild men; once children chased after the brothers poking at them with sticks. They returned to the Portiuncula as the autumn cold weather was setting in, disappointed but with their determination undimmed. A fire burned by the willow hut, and Francis greeted it with a cry of 'brother fire!' He treated everything that he encountered in the natural world as though it were part of his family: Brother Sun and

Sister Moon, Brother Wind and Sister Water, and, of course, Lady Poverty.

Five more recruits joined them before the end of the year, including two noblemen called Philip the Long and Angelo Tancredi. The people of Umbria watched with fascination as Francis drew people to him like a magnet. What was so appealing about the life of the brotherhood? It was unbelievably hard: apart from being barefoot and scarcely clothed in all weather, the brothers got up at midnight to pray.

In order that people should be clear about the intentions of the brotherhood, Francis wrote out a kind of statement of their purpose which he called the Rule. As the numbers of the brotherhood grew, there would be several more Rules – some of them got very bogged down in details and regulations which were certainly not what Francis had intended – but they always stuck fast to the two most important features: having no possessions at all and loving God above everything or anybody else – which meant finding God in everything and everybody.

Francis began to see that as the brotherhood grew, he would need the protection of the Pope, the head of the whole Christian Church. In the Middle Ages, it would have been almost unthinkable for religious groups to act independently of the Pope. Francis respected the authority of the Church and he wanted the brotherhood to be given a seal of approval from the Holy Father, the head of the Church. At that time there were a great many religious groups – most of them nuns and monks living in convents and monasteries. The groups were known as Orders. Francis realised that if he could persuade the Pope to give his brotherhood permission to call themselves an Order, they would have an official seal of approval. Some religious Orders were among the richest landowners in Europe but Francis's would be the exact opposite; and the brothers would be friars (which comes from the Latin word fratres which means brothers), and unlike monks they would not stay in one place, but travel about.

CHAPTER 6
Meeting the Pope

Pope Innocent III was an aristocrat – before he became Pope he had been a prince – and was admired for his iron discipline and sharp intellect. In appearance he was purse-lipped and stern and was once described, rather unfairly, as looking as though he 'lived on lemons'.

When he received a message that a young man from Assisi called Francis Bernadone wanted to come and see him about forming a new religious order, his heart sank. There were so many people trying to form new religious groups: all over Europe, people seemed to be getting rid of their belongings and trying to live according to the Gospel in the most exacting way. Only a few years ago, there had been a very popular group called

The Poor Men of Lyons for example, and then there were the Humiliati of Verona who also lived in extreme poverty.

In the Pope's opinion, something always went wrong with these high-minded fanatics and they all too often ended up in a state of confusion. Their ideals were too high, that was the problem. You can't expect people to be perfect in this world: it never works and it leads to trouble.

Innocent III was a pessimist: he was generally disposed to look upon human beings as miserable creatures who mostly got things wrong – the opposite of the way that Francis thought of them. The Pope did not live luxuriously himself: he did not eat a lot or particularly enjoy the rich trappings of the Lateran Palace where the popes lived. He was open-minded to change, tolerant of people who wanted to be different and he had a lot of sympathy with these people who longed for the freedom of poverty. But he couldn't let them all go wandering about the country willy-nilly – it was bad for the authority of the Church. So, as he sat on his throne in a great audience chamber, he wondered if Francis Bernadone would be any different from the rest of them.

When Francis entered, the Pope looked at him with

interest which soon turned to disgust. His visitor was so skinny and dirty, his bare feet calloused from tramping along rutted roads. His hair was caked with mud and he quite obviously hadn't shaved for a very long time. Francis was not an edifying spectacle.

The Pope felt impatient: if you come to ask the most powerful man in Christendom for a favour, then the very least you could do is wash and brush up. He thought he'd teach Francis a lesson, and said to him: 'Go and find some pigs, live in the pigsty and persuade them to live by your Rule. After all, you look more like a pig than a human being.' Then he waved his hand to indicate that Francis should leave immediately. He thought he might hear a word of protest. But NO, this funny little man simply smiled, turned round, and positively skipped out of the room!

A day or so later, Innocent learned that Francis had returned, that he had followed his orders and wished to have another interview. The doors opened and a terrible stench wafted into the audience chamber. There was Francis, beaming from ear to ear, and smeared all over with stinking pigs' dung which dripped off him onto the floor. Despite himself, the Pope was impressed and intrigued. This Francis fellow was certainly determined. He was not, however, going to have a close-up interview with anyone who smelt as awful as this. He agreed to meet Francis properly when he'd cleaned himself up.

He then summoned all 12 of the Assisi brotherhood and questioned them closely. Did they think they could stick to the harsh Rule they had imposed on themselves? What about those who might join and be unable to endure the hardship?

In his beautiful troubadour's voice, Francis told Pope Innocent a story about a benevolent king, a knightly hero and a beautiful maiden who eventually had a brood of splendid sons. It was a characteristically romantic way of Francis saying that he saw himself as the knight, wedded to the maiden Poverty and that the Pope was the kindly monarch who would permit them to marry and produce a great family for future generations. The Pope made the brothers go outside while he talked it over with his cardinals. Innocent couldn't help himself: he was as susceptible to the great warmth of Francis's charm as everyone else. At first, the cardinals were not at all sure but the Pope won them round. He liked Francis and admired him too: there was something joyful about him which you didn't expect to find in someone who had given up so much and lived in such discomfort. And, in addition to all

these reasons, the Pope had suddenly remembered a
dream he'd had the night before, in which his church,
the Lateran Church in Rome, had been on the edge of
complete collapse. The building had been supported
only by the shoulders of one slight, frail man with thick
black eyebrows.

From now on, the brotherhood at the Portiuncula would be a religious order under the protection of the Pope himself. They called themselves the Order of the Friars Minor.

CHAPTER 7
Brotherhood

There were a great many different kinds of characters among the brothers. In any other kind of community, so many contrasting personalities would have found it difficult not to quarrel. But though they must occasionally have got on each others' nerves, Francis's brothers were so interested in being part of Francis's new movement, that they usually forgot their differences and remembered only the aim they all shared.

Francis's first companion, Brother Bernard, was always quiet and solitary; he liked to spend hours alone in prayer. In that way he was similar to Brother Rufino who 'prayed even in his sleep'. Brother Lucido had the same roaming urge and itchy feet as Francis and didn't like to linger too long in the same place. Brother Masseo was practical and commonsensical. Brother Leo, a priest, was wise and became the closest of them all to Francis. Then there was Brother Juniper who was sunny, innocent and loving. Even Francis was amazed at Juniper's passion for giving things away – not least the silver from the Portiuncula church – but he admired him, once saying 'I wish I had a forest of such junipers'.

Near the city of Ancona, Francis had met a wiry young boy who could turn double somersaults and juggle. He was a French tumbler, a jongleur, which is a French name for a travelling acrobat. Francis loved him immediately and when the tumbler wanted to join the brothers, he was delighted. He gave him a new name, Pacificus, and liked to have him near him all the time because he made him laugh. Pacificus had some interestingly colourful visions. These are not quite the same as dreams as they don't appear while you're asleep, but while you are awake and (usually) in a trance. Pacificus once saw a cross on Francis's forehead that gave off bright colours like a kaleidoscope.

***

The numbers of brothers went on growing. From all over Italy, young men came to join the Friars Minor and then left to preach all over the country, making even more converts along the way. Francis was not always an easy person to follow. Despite his gentleness, you needed to be passionate and single-minded to keep up with what he demanded. He ate very little and refused to sleep on the straw-filled pads used by the other brothers, preferring to feel the hard bumps of the ground underneath him. He once spent the 40 days of Lent alone on an island in Lake Trasimene and, in all that time, ate only half a loaf of bread. Yet at the same time, Francis took a dim view of brothers who behaved as though they wanted a gold medal for suffering. This was not a competition. Although all the men wore scratchy jerkins known as 'hair shirts' that were deliberately made to be uncomfortable, Francis was furious when he found that some of the men were also wearing iron implements that cut into their skin for extra pain.

Wearing hair shirts and eating very little (known as fasting) were not supposed to be a tests of strength to see who could last out longest: they were intended to make one feel more alive and to concentrate the heart. He didn't tolerate friars who behaved unkindly to each other and on one occasion he made Brother Barbaro eat asses' dung for speaking angrily to another brother.

At times his sense of humour could be difficult to understand too – like the time when he was out preaching on the road with Brother Masseo and spun him round and round until he was dizzy before making him point in the direction in which they were to go. And he once ordered Brother Rufino, who was particularly shy, to go and preach naked in the centre of Assisi.

All the brothers had different ways of keeping themselves from being distracted by temptations for things they couldn't have. For each of them had made different sacrifices to be part of the brotherhood at Portiuncula. For Francis, the most difficult thing was knowing that he had given up the chance of ever having a wife and family. Many of his companions later remembered that when he found himself thinking about it too much, he threw himself into a snowdrift shouting 'this is for my wife!', and then, throwing himself down again, 'this is for my son!' Brother Juniper, when he pondered too long on how nice it would be to give up the rough ground and have a more comfortable bed, would simply run around the fields very fast until the feeling went away.

At each new town the friars entered, the church bells rang out and children greeted them waving olive tree branches. The news spread that this strange, threadbare man called Francis could miraculously cure the most terrible illnesses. There were rumours that very sick people had been completely cured by eating bread that had been blessed by Francis. In fact, so many people snipped off pieces of his tunic in the hope that they might bring them good luck that it very often had more holes than cloth.

There are many, many stories of Francis working miracles: he gave sight to a blind woman, he made a cripple walk again; he straightened the twisted hands of a woman with arthritis. One day, Francis was walking alone along a mountain road when a woman rushed in front of him begging him to cure her dying baby. When he saw the child, he seemed to recognise something in its face and he cried 'O buona ventura!' – which means 'welcome'. The baby survived and it was christened Bonaventure. Later he became leader of all the brotherhood and wrote a life of Francis. Many of Francis's miracles are playful – in the way that he too was playful. One time, he was praying with such concentration that solid, down-to-earth Brother Masseo, standing just behind him, was lifted clear off the ground by Francis's breath – as if he were a feather.

***

Among the most famous stories about Francis are those concerning animals. He was particularly at home when talking to animals and birds. Once, while he was giving a sermon in a field, Francis asked the swallows to stop interrupting him with their twittering – and they immediately fell silent.

Probably the most famous picture of Francis shows him giving his celebrated 'sermon to the birds'. It is painted by Giotto, and if you ever visit the Church of St Francis at Assisi you will see it there. It depicts Francis talking earnestly to a row of birds sitting in the branches of an oak tree. They appear to be listening to him intently. According to the story, Francis was out walking when he suddenly hopped into a field, telling his astonished companions that he was going to preach a sermon to the birds. When he began speaking, the birds gathered about him completely unafraid, some of them sitting on his head and shoulders. Of all the birds, the ones he loved the most were larks, which nest in fields, scavenge in dung heaps, and soar wildly upward, singing in a delicious crescendo. He often thought of himself as a lark with its ugly, dark plumage and its beautiful song.

There are so many stories of Francis and animals that it is quite difficult to work out which ones are true. There is, for example, one story of a hare who became so tame after she heard Francis speak that she lolloped after him wherever he went. And there was a rabbit who put her head in his lap; and another story about some turtle doves he saved from being eaten, which then refused to fly away from him. Then there is the celebrated story of the vicious wolf which came down from the forests and terrorised the town of Gubbio. Francis apparently visited the wolf who listened meekly as he ordered it to stop eating people. And he told the people of Gubbio to give the wolf regular meals. For the next two years, before the wolf died, it meekly went from door to door in Gubbio with its head bowed, waiting for its next feed.

Francis didn't love all animals in quite the same way. He was never very fond of mice because they lived in the rough straw mattresses on which the brothers slept and nibbled them in the night. He also thought pigs were dirty and that ants were boring because, with their constant hoarding of stores of food and worrying about the future, they reminded him of busy accountants (and maybe his father Pietro the canny merchant).

CHAPTER 8
Clare

Hundreds of men from all over Italy wanted to be part of Francis's extraordinary new movement, but the most important, the most famous, of his followers was actually a woman. She became Francis's closest, most beloved, friend, though they never once spent more than one hour at a time alone in one another's company.

Her name was Clare di Offreduccio, (Chiara in Italian) and she was born into one of Assisi's noblest families. She spent her early childhood in exile with her parents in Perugia – during the time when Francis was a prisoner of war. The family returned to Assisi as he was beginning his wanderings. From the windows of their large house, the Offreduccios would have watched with interest Francis's dramatic renunciation of his father; they would have heard of the conversion of Bernard of Quintavalle.

By the time Clare first saw him preach in Assisi, Francis was the city's most famous citizen; he was already one of the most talked-about men in Italy. Clare liked Francis's shabbiness, his passion and his courage. She listened to him speaking in public and watched him closely. She fell in love with Francis long before they met.

Clare knew that she wanted to share Francis's upside-down life. The future that her family had planned for her – which included marriage to a wealthy man, lots of children and several servants – now seemed tedious and uninviting. Clare didn't want to be another lonely rich woman trapped behind the high windows of her big house. She longed for the romantic adventure and freedom of real poverty. To the surprise and concern of her family, she began visiting the poorest inhabitants of Assisi and the lepers in the leprosaria. Then her cousin Rufino slipped quietly away to join Francis's brotherhood in the woods.

Francis was afraid of falling in love – he felt particularly vulnerable to it. He had tricks by which he avoided women in case he felt too attracted to them. If he happened to pass near a woman, he kept his head down and was careful not to look them in the face. So when Brother Rufino introduced him to Clare Offreduccio, he was on his guard. But Clare was different because, like Francis, she was unconventional. Within an hour of meeting her, he knew that here was someone who shared his vision. Soon he found that they were talking excitedly about love – the love of God and truth. They were true companions.

They met again, and again, and they went on talking and sharing plans. Their meetings were always secret and took place in the woods at night. But they were never alone together: Francis was always accompanied by Brother Philip and Clare came with her cousins Pacifica or Bona Offreduccio. If Clare's family had known she was slipping out of the house at night to meet with Francis, they would have been terrified of losing her to this strange world below the city, where men chose to live in huts and beg for food. They would have been horrified to think that she might give up everything to go and live with men at all: in those days, women never talked to men alone unless they were closely related to them.

Clare was desperate to join Francis's brotherhood, though Francis himself was more dubious. He had a rather fairytale, romantic notion of women and wasn't sure he liked the idea of Clare living in poverty and begging for food like the brothers. But Clare was determined, and she convinced Francis that she could never be happy unless she too was living the life of the brotherhood. Francis, of course, was always excited by the thought of an adventure. He gradually came round to the idea although, as usual, he considered the practicalities after the event. They planned that Clare would run away to join Francis on Palm Sunday, which is one week before Easter Sunday.

In the middle of the night, when the Offreduccios were asleep, Clare slipped out of the house with Pacifica and walked hurriedly down the moonlit hillside to the woods and the Portiuncula. Francis and some of the other brothers were there to meet them. Clare handed them her expensive clothes and jewels and put on a rough habit tied with a cord. She swore an oath of obedience to the Order. Her long hair was then cut off close to her head in a spiky thatch. If you visit Assisi, you can go to the church there which is dedicated to Clare. There you will see a lock of her hair that was cut off that night. It is blonde and wavy and preserved in a casket.

Now the important part of the adventure was over

and it was time to face up to the hard facts. Brother Rufino knew that his family would be scandalised if Clare went to live as the only woman in the woods. He knew furthermore that if they didn't act fast, the Offreduccio men would soon arrive to grab her back. So Francis made a quick decision: although Clare pleaded to stay with him, he dispatched her to a near-by convent.

Four days later, her family tracked her down and her furious cousins rode down to the convent. They told her she had behaved badly, that she had embarrassed the whole family, but when they tried to drag her back with them, she clung to the chapel altar. Then she pushed back her hood and showed them her shaven head.

When they saw it, they gave up their attempts to make her return. The cropping of a woman's hair was one of the most important signs of her commitment to a religious life – and if you had decided to live a religious life, no one was permitted to stop you.

But Clare didn't want to be yet another nun in a wealthy convent: she had joined Francis's order and she was determined to keep her promise to him: to live in absolute poverty like his friars. Francis and some of the brothers then came to fetch her away to another, poorer, convent up in the mountains. A week later, her 14-year-old sister Caterina ran away to join her, taking the new name of Agnes. With the women of the family all apparently running off to live like Francis Bernadone, the Offreduccios thought their world was crumblng around them. They also tried to drag Agnes back, pulling her physically across the floor of the convent until she fainted. But she too refused to return.

***

Eventually the Bishop (the same bishop who had passed judgement on Francis and his father four years before) intervened. He gave to Clare and Agnes the church at San Damiano where they could live under Francis's Rule – although they agreed not to go out preaching or begging, but to remain always inside the building.

Clare had longed to be a holy wanderer like Francis and his brothers, but in the world of the Middle Ages, it was impossible to imagine women roaming unprotected about the countryside. So Clare remained enclosed at San Damiano for the rest of her life. But it was not long before many other women were clamouring to join her and Agnes, including a third

Offreduccio sister, Beatrice, and Clare's mother Ortolana.

Clare did not see Francis often but they never stopped loving each other. There are many legends concerning Clare and Francis's love. In one of them, Francis told Clare that it was just too difficult and painful for them to go on being friends. In an over-the-top way typical of him, he said they should never see each other again and, pointing dramatically at a dead bush, cried: 'when that bush blooms, then we will meet again'. Instantly, the dry twigs sprouted perfect roses.

Another story tells how Clare begged to be allowed to eat a meal with Francis. For ages, he sternly refused though finally he invited her to share a meal with the brothers. Apparently, the people of Assisi looking down into the woods saw a blazing light shining from the place where Francis and Clare sat talking together of the love of God.

Clare herself had intense visions, often so vivid that they seemed three dimensional. This is why, in the twentieth century, she was made the patron saint of television.

***

Clare and the women who lived at San Damiano were known as the Poor Ladies. The Pope gave them the official status of Order and this still exists – its members are now known as the Poor Clares. They lived in strictest frugality, eating little and sleeping only a few hours every night. But Clare filled her garden with flowers and Francis liked to come and sit there in the summer. It was in this spot that he composed his lovely poem 'The Song to Brother Sun'.

CHAPTER 9
Meeting the Sultan

In 1212, the same year that Clare settled at San Damiano, Francis made the first of his two attempts to reach the Middle East. He had never forgotten his early ambition to be a Crusader, to liberate the holy city of Jerusalem from the Saracens. As we saw earlier, his efforts to be soldier had so far failed dismally, but Francis still believed that to fight and, with any luck, to die for your faith was the greatest thing a man could be called upon to do. He was to learn that it was not quite that straightforward.

For people living in Europe in the Middle Ages, Palestine, which they called the Holy Land, was the centre of the known world. Thousands trekked across the continent to Jerusalem on pilgrimages to the Holy

Places – which marked the important locations in the life of Jesus. Jerusalem, then as now, was in fact the site of three great faiths: Judaism, Islam and Christianity. All these religions regarded it as their city – which has been the cause of many wars.

It was the goal of all European Christians to take back control of Jerusalem from the Saracens who had conquered it in 1187. Every boy aspired to be a Crusader and sail to Jerusalem to fight. The reality was not so romantic. In the same year that Francis made his first journey, a teenage Spanish shepherd led over 50,000 children across Europe towards Palestine. It was known as The Children's Crusade. Not one of the children ever reached their destination: on the way, they died of disease, exhaustion, starvation or were captured by slave-traders.

Francis, as we have seen, shared this romantic fantasy of the Crusaders' life. And so it was that he embarked on the first of his own crusades. Acting on one of his usual spontaneous impulses, he set off with one companion to the Adriatic Sea, on the east coast of Italy, where he begged a place on a ship heading to Syria. The ship ran into a storm and when it finally limped to land on the coast of Croatia, the captain threw the passengers out.

Francis decided to head back home but failed to find a ship that would give them free passage. They therefore had to stow away in a hold used for storing rope and barrels. Some days later, hungry sailors discovered the stowaways and also found that the men's supply of food had been mysteriously replenished even though there was nothing left on board to eat. The sailors hailed the stowaways with loud jubilation at this miracle and, so the story goes, the ship sailed on to Italy with all its passengers well fed and happy.

Two years later, Francis decided to go to Morocco to meet the leader of the Muslim Moors – which was what the Moroccans, who then ruled most of southern Spain, were known as. He got as far as Spain, then collapsed with exhaustion and had to walk back to Italy. It looked as though every time Francis wanted to go on a Crusade, something happened to stop him.

***

In 1215, Pope Innocent III called a mighty Council of the Church. He made a stirring speech, calling for a new Crusade to win back the Holy Sepulchre in Jerusalem, the holiest of all the Christian Holy Places. It was another four years before Francis took up the challenge. He walked towards the coast accompanied by a large crowd of brothers all eager to go crusading too.

When they arrived at the port, he turned to them, laughed, and said he couldn't possibly take them all. He called over a small boy playing on the quayside: 'come here and choose 12 of these men for me'. To the brothers' consternation the boy picked out the ones

allowed to go with Francis. At every port at which their ship stopped, there were thousands of Crusaders primed for battle, waiting for ships, crammed into hostelries, not sure exactly where they were going. It seemed very disorganised.

They sailed to the great city of Acre in Syria, a staging-post for hopeful Crusaders. But Francis was deeply disappointed by what he found there. He saw Crusaders, who should have been the models of courtesy and gentleness, drunk, rowdy and rude to the people of the city. There were lazy and indolent priests and sleazy traders telling gullible, just-arrived, Crusaders that scraps of wood and bone were holy relics – pieces of the True Cross on which Jesus had been crucified, or pieces of a saint's bone that would bring good luck. The great Crusader King Andrew of Hungary had recently bought an old pot, which he was persuaded was actually one of the casks which held the water that Jesus miraculously turned into wine at the wedding feast in Cana.

But Francis pressed on. His aim was now to reach Damietta in Egypt, where the Crusaders had for months been besieging the city. The Sultan of Egypt, Melek-al-Kamil, was the nephew of Saladin himself, the leader of the Saracens. The Sultan had been forced to set up camp six miles further down the River Nile.

***

Many things surprised Francis when he arrived in Damietta. For one thing, there were many European Christians then living in Egypt who didn't want to fight the Saracens – war was bad for the peaceful trading relations which had been established there. He found too that the city of Damietta had been completely destroyed by the Crusaders: there had once been 80,000 inhabitants – now there were only 3,000. He was shocked to find, as in Acre, that many of the Crusaders were looting and brawling. What is more, at one point, when the Sultan actually offered to surrender to the Crusaders the whole of Jerusalem and many of the Christian sites in Palestine, the Crusaders couldn't seem to agree on what they wanted. Many of them, including Churchmen, actually wanted to fight on until the Saracens were completely crushed and obliterated. Francis was deeply disturbed by this glorying in bloodshed.

***

It was fearfully hot in fly-ridden Damietta and tempers were frayed by long hours of waiting for something to happen. Francis must have struck the soldiers as a peculiar sight among the fluttering banners of a military camp. Dressed in his shabby robe, he walked among the hardened men, kneeling to talk to the sick, wounded and starving. He was sickened when the soldiers, weary of their leaders arguing among themselves, launched a sudden attack on the enemy themselves. The death toll was horrific: 4,300 men killed in one day. Francis had desperately tried to warn the soldiers against it, but they had dismissed him as a madman and a fool.

The Sultan went on offering terms of peace. He would give the Crusaders Jerusalem, a portion of the Holy Land and the region of the Lake of Galilee, where Jesus and his disciples had come from. He offered to return many of the Crusaders' captured castles. And he agreed to a truce, or a ceasefire, for 30 years.

Francis was determined to meet the Sultan. Maybe he could convert him, win him over with the charm and enthusiasm which had been so successful in Italy. And if the Sultan had him bloodily murdered? Well then, he would have died honourably for his faith. A cardinal, based in Damietta, advised him strongly not to attempt such a dangerous mission but Francis, as usual, would not be put off. He set out for the Sultan's camp at Fariskur with one companion, Brother Illuminato. When they reached the gates, the guards, amazed at the sight of these two shabby figures striding brazenly towards them, knocked them to the floor, kicking them about. But the two men called out 'Sultan! Sultan!' and the guards let them go. Perhaps Melek al Kamil heard them shouting and asked for them to be let in. No-one knows how it came about but they were granted an interview.

If Francis had been expecting his enemy to look fierce and warlike, he must have been very surprised. The Sultan was a man of Francis's own age, with a mild, intelligent manner and a good-humoured twinkle in his eye. He was cultured and particularly enjoyed reading poetry. Naturally, he was intrigued by Francis, and looked quizzically at this odd, brave man, with his burning sincerity and his laughing eyes.

First of all, the men engaged in a battle of wits. The Sultan thought he could test Francis by ordering him to walk aross a carpet covered with a pattern of crosses. To tread on a symbol of Jesus's Cross would have been considered a terrible insult to Christians. But Francis was quick off the mark: he cunningly observed that

Christians had the Cross of Jesus in their possession, so any cross that might be found on the Sultan's carpet would have to illustrate the crosses on which the two thieves were crucified on either side of Jesus. Therefore, Francis announced, he would happily walk over the carpet.

The Sultan liked Francis's style and listened to him with respect. Francis, however, was still determined to put on a dramatic display that would prove to the Sultan once and for all the absolute truth of Christianity. He proposed an ordeal by fire. This was a tradition in both religions and involved the very frightening practice of walking through a blazing fire that, if it left you unmarked, would prove that your religion was the true one.

Francis suggested that he and Illuminato would walk through fire at the same time as two Islamic clerics, and they would see which of them got burned. Fortunately, the Sultan's clerics, seeing all sorts of problems with such an extreme challenge, refused to take it up. Francis's grand gesture rather fizzled out. Then he offered to go through the fire alone – the deal being that the Sultan must promise that he and his people would convert to Christianity if Francis survived the ordeal without a mark. But the Sultan still refused, reminding Francis that there would be a revolt among the Saracens if he ordered them all to change their religion.

After all that, there was nothing left to do but for Francis to return to his own side. But he and Melek-al-Kamil had a sense that a friendship had been forged between them. Francis respected the Sultan and the Sultan respected Francis. The Arabs pressed gifts of gold, silk and silver on the friars – which they refused, but they returned to the Crusaders at Damietta with a Saracen guard to protect them.

CHAPTER 10
The final years

F rancis had to hurry back from Egypt (well, as far as you can hurry when you are walking almost all the way). He had heard disturbing news about the Order while he was away. The brothers who had been running matters in his absence had tampered with his Rule, introducing the kind of petty regulations that Francis most disliked, obsessing over the details which mattered least. They had even tried to ban the eating of all meat, milk, eggs and cheese.

On his way home, he visited his friars in the Italian city of Bologna and found they had built a centre of learning there, a library full of books and students. You might think this was a good idea, but Francis was furious: it had nothing to do with the revolution of prayer, preaching and poverty that he had intended. There was worse to come when he reached his beloved church of the Portiuncula: it had been roofed with expensive new tiles. He was so angry that he climbed on the roof and hurled the tiles to the ground.

The Order had so many members that it appeared to be slipping beyond Francis's influence and becoming an unwieldy bureaucracy. It was growing at an impressive rate and there were missions to all the countries of Europe – including England. But although Francis had inspired and formed it, in many ways it no longer felt as though it were his beloved brotherhood.

***

Three years after those first twelve men had set off to see the Pope, the number of Francis's friars had swelled to 300. To keep an eye on what was happening with them all, Francis held a meeting at the Portiuncula twice a year. This meeting was known as a chapter. From all over Europe, barefoot figures in grey robes trudged over mountains and across plains to attend. And every year, there were more and more of them.

In 1217, Cardinal Ugolino looked down from the walls of Assisi over a vast expanse of willow huts, laid

out like rush mats on the plains below. Five thousand friars had assembled for what became known in later years as the Chapter of Mats. The Cardinal found the spectacle so moving that he took off his rich cloak and shoes and processed humbly to Mass behind the brothers. Thousands of local people bringing carts full of food and drink added to the numbers. As the Cardinal observed, 'truly this is a camp and the army of the knights of God'.

Although he was not yet 40, Francis was increasingly frail. He sought more solitude, spending days, weeks, months alone, deep in conversation with God. His eyes became diseased and soon he could barely see. In the thirteenth century, the medical treatments frequently caused more suffering than the illness. The doctors prescribed cauterisation for Francis's eyes – which means branding with a red-hot iron. As the iron approached, his poor companion brothers had to look away because they couldn't bear it. But Francis addressed the branding iron as if it were a friend, murmuring: 'Deal gently with me, Brother Fire, for I have always been very courteous with you.'

Three years after his return from Egypt, Francis spent Christmas in the small Italian town of Greccio. There he had the idea of re-enacting the scenes of Bethlehem – the stable, the manger, Joseph, Mary and Jesus – on a snowy hillside outside the town.

News spread of the re-enactment and on the bright, cold midnight of Christmas Eve, hundreds of people from all over Italy carried torches and candles in procession up the hill. There Francis celebrated a Mass surrounded by oxen, donkeys and sheep – the animals which would have been in the stable at Bethlehem. Though he was tired and ill, something of Francis's old passion came back that night and people never forgot how powerful his words were. This was his call to revolution: give up everything that the world calls valuable – for love.

Not entirely consistent with his own preaching, Francis did once accept a magnificent gift. In 1213, he had been given by a nobleman an entire mountain about 50 miles from Assisi. Alverna, as it is called, is a high, rocky, wooded peak, studded with caves. It became a very important place for Francis and now he spent long periods in a cave on Alverna. He spoke to no-one, and a brother crossed a rope bridge to leave him some thin gruel once a day. On one occasion, Brother Leo, walking away from the bridge, saw, hovering over Francis's cave, an angel with six shining wings.

***

Francis retired from the world, like a troubadour who now sang only in his imagination. And he resigned as Head of the Order: from now on, let the brotherhood of friars, with its complicated rules, its politics, sub-divisions and distractions, look after itself.

It was in the cave at Alverna that Francis received the

stigmata. This means that in his hands, his feet and his side he developed five open wounds identical to those that Jesus suffered when he was crucified. In the intense solitude and holiness of Alverna, Francis's sympathy with Jesus had made him, literally, experience his wounds. But the agony in his feet now made it impossible for him to walk, and he was brought back to Assisi on the back of a donkey. For some time, wracked with pain, he sat every day in Clare's garden at San Damiano, where he added a new verse to his poem to Brother Sun – it was a greeting to Sister Death.

It took Francis a long time to die. But one evening, he asked his loyal brothers to carry him to the woods and lie him down on the earth near the Portiuncula. The city watchmen of Assisi later reported that they had been amazed to see hundreds of larks circling the Portiuncula and singing clamorously.

There, under the trees, on 12 October 1226, he died. Francis had once asked to be buried in the most despised plot in Assisi – the place where criminals were taken to be executed. But his followers instead took his body back to the city to be buried in the Church of St George. They were followed by hundreds of people carrying olive branches. Rich, poor, beggars, lepers, priests, minstrels and merchants – all of them wanted to have a last glimpse of Francis. The procession stopped at San Damiano where Clare kissed Francis's hands through the open grille in the door which enclosed her.

***

Two years after Francis's death, in 1228, he was canonised, which means that the Pope officially pronounced him to be a saint – St Francis of Assisi. The moment that the news of Francis's death left the city, Assisi had been swamped by pilgrims. It was important to build a secure new tomb it was quite common in the Middle Ages for pilgrims to try and take bits of the body as holy relics.

The day after Francis's canonisation, Pope Gregory IX (the successor to Innocent III) laid the foundation stone for an enormous church in Assisi to honour the new saint. This ragged, gentle, light-hearted man who had once been mocked as 'il pazzo' had changed the face of Europe. The ceremony was attended by thousands of Friars Minor (nowadays called Franciscans after their founder) who watched as the body of their founder St Francis was re-buried deep within the church named after him.

TIMELINE

1181 – Giovanni Bernadone born in Assisi, in the Spoleto Valley.

1187 – Jerusalem falls to Saladin at the Battle of the Horns of Hattin.

1198 – The death of Celestine III and the election of Pope Innocent III.

1198 – Conrad of Urslingen, the German ruler of Spoleto left the valley and his Italian holdings to be taken over by the papacy which now asserted its power of the German empire.

1202-4 – Francis in prison in Perugia

1205 – Abortive mission to Spoleto, depressed, comes back determined to work for the poor. On the way back sees speaking crucifix

1206 – Goes to Foligno having stolen his father's cloth. Horrified by very fact of money. Falls out with his father, and becomes a hermit.

1209 – Hears the New Testament gospel and knows he must preach perfection. (p54 Smith)

1209 – Albigensian crusade and Innocent III clamps down on the Cathars, horribly. "The Perfect men"

1212 – St Clare joins order

1215 – Fourth lateran Council

1219 – Chapter of Mats

1224 – Greccio and the stable/crib

1226 – Francis dies

QUIZ

After you've finished the book, test yourself and see how well you remember what you've read.

1. As a boy, Giovanni Bernadone was known as 'Il Francesco' because:
   He had a large collection of French francs
   He was always honest and frank
   He liked to sing the songs he learned in France

2. Before he set off for the Crusades, Francis decided to:
   Get some experience as a soldier in southern Italy
   Have a holiday with his mates on the Riviera
   Train in hand-to-hand combat at the local barracks

3. What title was Francis given by his friends?
   Prince of Darkness
   King of the Revels
   Lord of the Rings

4. On 5 February 1207 Francis repaid his father what he had stolen in order to restore the church at San Damiano and:
   Stripped off all his clothes and renounced his rights as a son
   Got down on his knees and begged for forgiveness
   Burst into a song about his love for Lady Poverty

5. In the 13th century, travelling singers were known as:
   Martians
   Maltesers
   Minstrels

6. When Francis discovered one of his followers had accepted a gift of money, he instructed him to:

    Buy a new suit of clothes and a hot meal for every leper in the town

    Pick the money up in his mouth and drop it in a dung-heap

    Donate it to the Assisi Dogs' Home

7. Francis and his followers marked their scratchy grey tunics with:

    The peace symbol

    The sign of the cross

    A picture of a bird

8. When the Pope told Francis he looked like a pig and should go and live in a pigsty, he:

    Stormed off and sulked for two days

    Went off happily to obey the Pope's command

    Went straight to the barber's to have a wash and a haircut

9. The people who followed Francis's Rules were known as:

    Brovaz

    Big Brothers

    The Brotherhood

10. When Brother Barbaro spoke angrily to someone, Francis made him:

    Spin round and round until he was dizzy

    Eat asses' dung

    Preach naked in the centre of Assisi

11. What did Francis tell the people of Gubbio to do to the wolf that terrorised them?

    Make it the town mayor

Feed it regularly
Sing songs to it three times a day

12. Clare Offreduccio showed her determination to join Francis and his followers by:
    Cutting her long hair
    Refusing to take her exams
    Throwing a water bomb at the Bishop of Assisi

13. Because of her intense 3D visions, Clare was made the patron saint of:
    IMAX cinemas
    Kaleidoscopes
    Television

14. Francis found the Crusaders in Syria were:
    Drunk, rowdy and rude
    Courteous, gentle and devout
    Brave, intelligent and modest

15. The Sultan of Egypt set Francis a test to see if he could:
    Walk across a carpet
    Walk on water
    Walk on his hands

16. When Francis found his beloved church of the Portiuncula had expensive new tiles, he:
    Expressed his pleasure by singing his song to Brother Sun
    Hurled the tiles to the ground in a fit of anger
    Made some holes in the roof so the birds could shelter in bad weather

17. How many monks attended the Chapter of the Mats in 1217?

500
5000
50000

18. In the town of Greccio, Francis staged a:
    Breathtaking demonstration of stunt bike somersaults
    Stunning performance of the Lion King
    Moving re-enactment of the Nativity

19. Although Francis had vowed to have no possessions, he did once decide to accept a gift of:
    A mountain
    An elephant
    A pair of Birkenstocks

20. Francis asked his followers to bury him:
    In the church of San Damiano
    In his cave on Alverna
    In the execution ground of Assisi